THIS JOURNAL BELONGS TO:

_____

_____

Published by Christian Art Publishers
PO Box 1599, Vereeniging, 1930, RSA

© 2019
First edition 2019

Designed by Christian Art Publishers

Cover designed by Christian Art Publishers

Images used under license from Shutterstock.com

Printed in China

ISBN 978-1-4321-3076-3

21 22 23 24 25 26 27 28 29 30 – 12 11 10 9 8 7 6 5 4 3

My GRATITUDE Journal

CHRISTIAN ART
PUBLISHERS

G — God, grace, gifts, goodness, giving, gentleness, generosity, gardens, goals, grandparents, gatherings, glasses

R — roses, rain, righteousness, rest, rainbows, reading, relationships, relatives, retreats, rewards, rivers, roads, romance

A — apples, acceptance, adventures, airplanes, almonds, animals, anniversaries, art, assistance, aunts

T — travel, trees, teachers, time, talent, tea, telephones, traditions, tulips, tuna

I — ideas, inspiration, ice, islands, ice-cream, instruments, insects, Internet

T — teamwork, truth, trust, toast, trains, treasures, trips, trumpets, turkeys, technology, tennis

U — unity, umbrellas, universe, understanding, uniqueness, us, universities

D — dreams, discernment, dads, diaries, daughters, deer, dogs, donkeys, desserts, devotion, discipleship, dolphins, doctors, directions, daisies

E — encouragement, earth, examples, eagles, eggs, education, electricity, employment

Rejoice always,
pray continually,
GIVE
thanks
in all circumstances;
for this is God's will
for you in
CHRIST JESUS.

1 Thessalonians 5:16-18

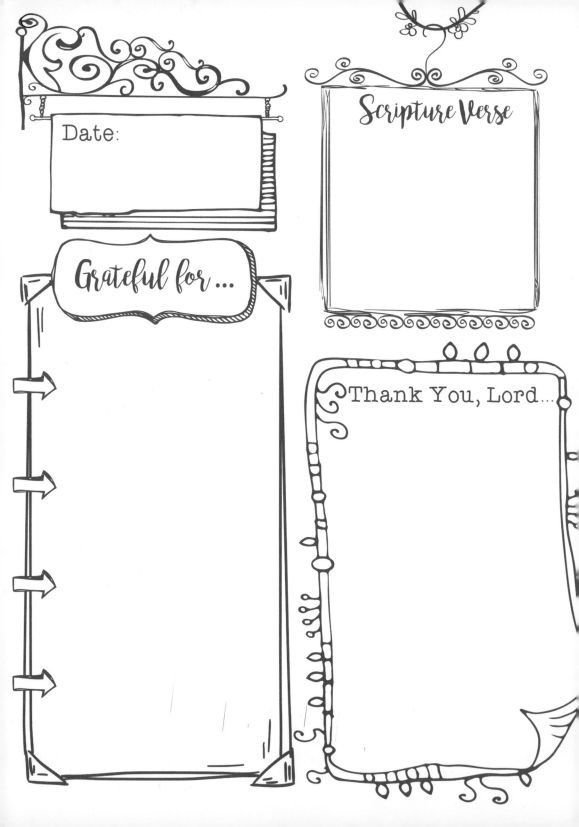

Date:

Scripture Verse

Grateful for ...

Thank You, Lord...

Date:

Scripture Verse

Grateful for ...

Thank You, Lord...

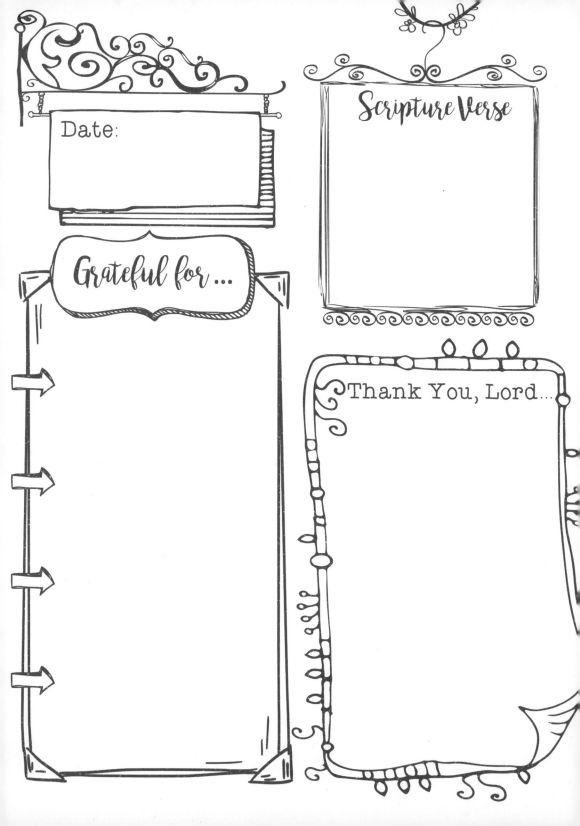

Date:

Scripture Verse

Grateful for ...

Thank You, Lord...

Date:

Scripture Verse

Grateful for ...

Thank You, Lord...

Date:

Scripture Verse

Grateful for ...

Thank You, Lord...

Date:

Scripture Verse

Grateful for ...

Thank You, Lord...

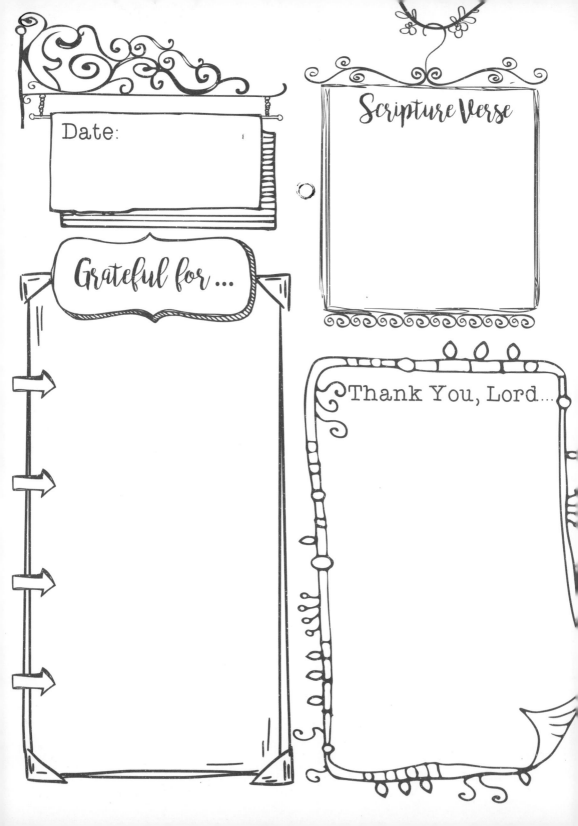

Date:

Scripture Verse

Grateful for ...

Thank You, Lord...

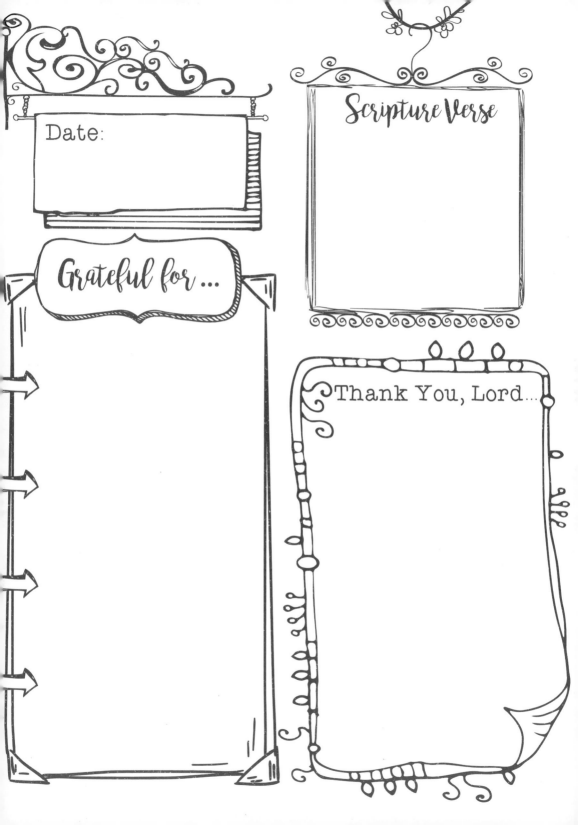

Date:

Scripture Verse

Grateful for ...

Thank You, Lord...

Date:

Scripture Verse

Grateful for ...

Thank You, Lord...

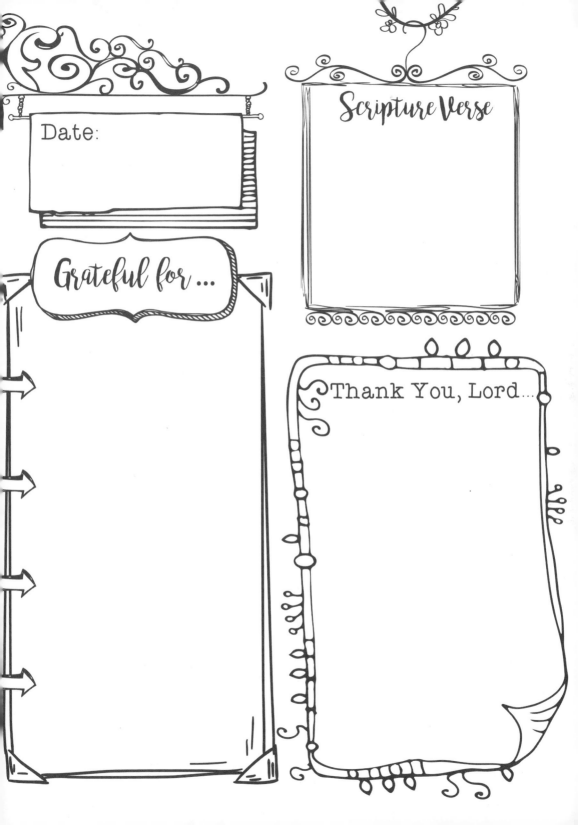

Date:

Scripture Verse

Grateful for ...

Thank You, Lord...

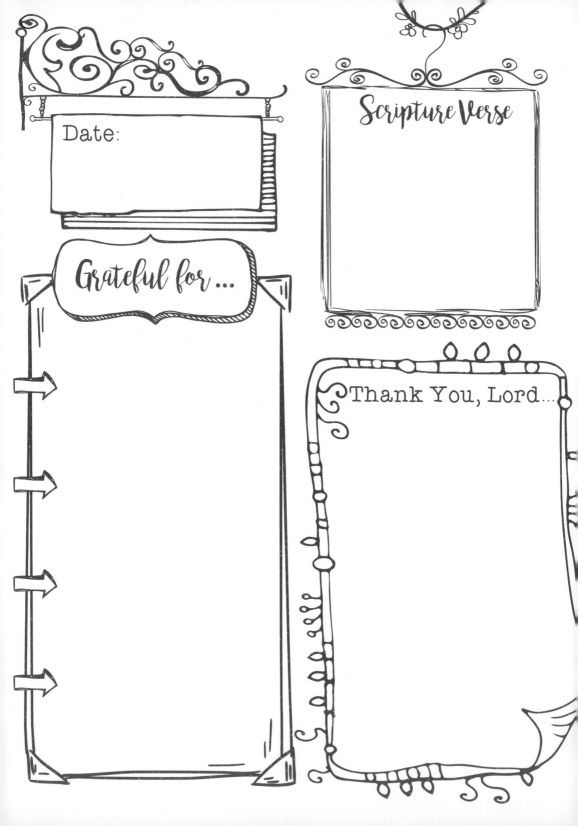

Date:

Scripture Verse

Grateful for ...

Thank You, Lord...

Date:

Scripture Verse

Grateful for ...

Thank You, Lord...

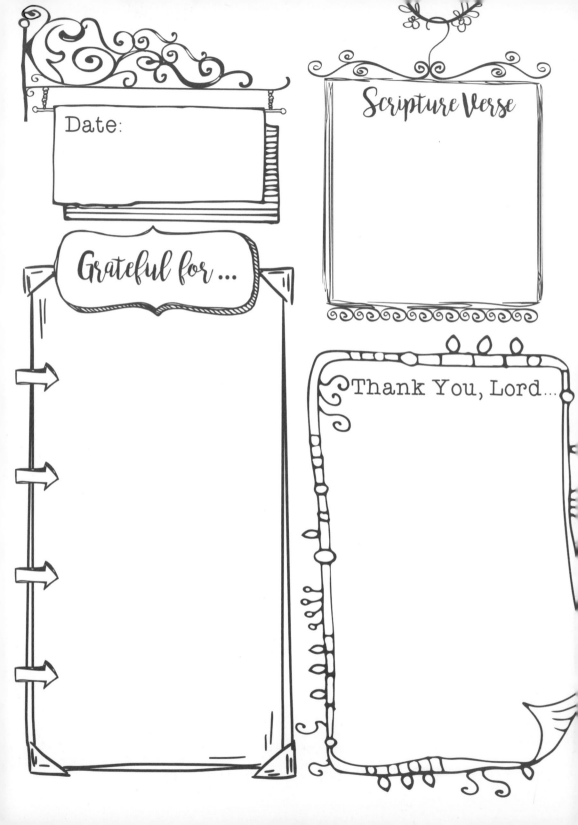

Date:

Scripture Verse

Grateful for ...

Thank You, Lord...

Date:

Scripture Verse

Grateful for ...

Thank You, Lord...

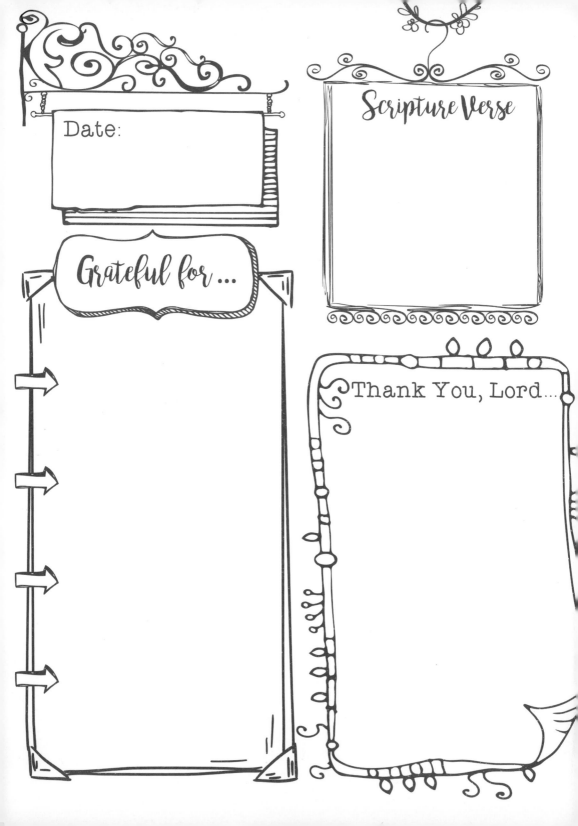

Date:

Scripture Verse

Grateful for ...

Thank You, Lord...

Date:

Scripture Verse

Grateful for ...

Thank You, Lord...

Date:

Scripture Verse

Grateful for ...

Thank You, Lord...

Date:

Scripture Verse

Grateful for ...

Thank You, Lord...

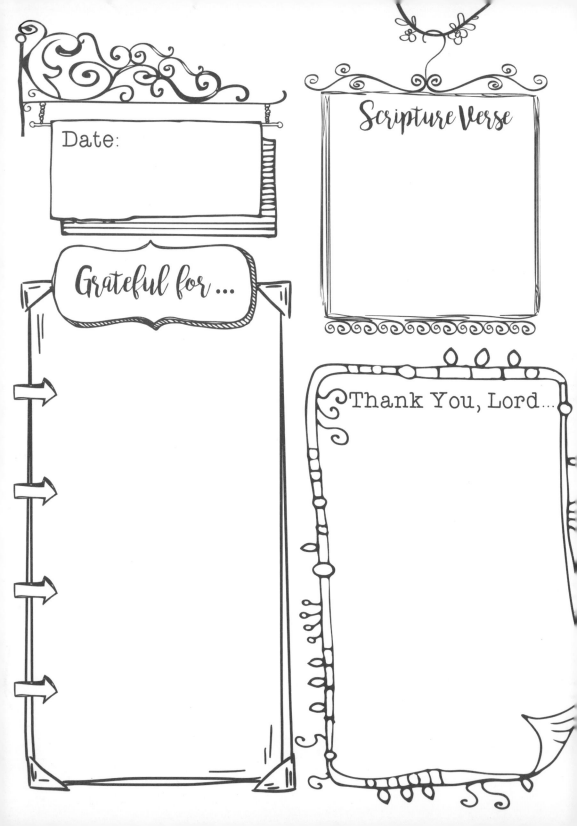

Date:

Scripture Verse

Grateful for ...

Thank You, Lord...

Date:

Scripture Verse

Grateful for ...

Thank You, Lord...

Date:

Scripture Verse

Grateful for ...

Thank You, Lord...

Date:

Scripture Verse

Grateful for ...

Thank You, Lord...

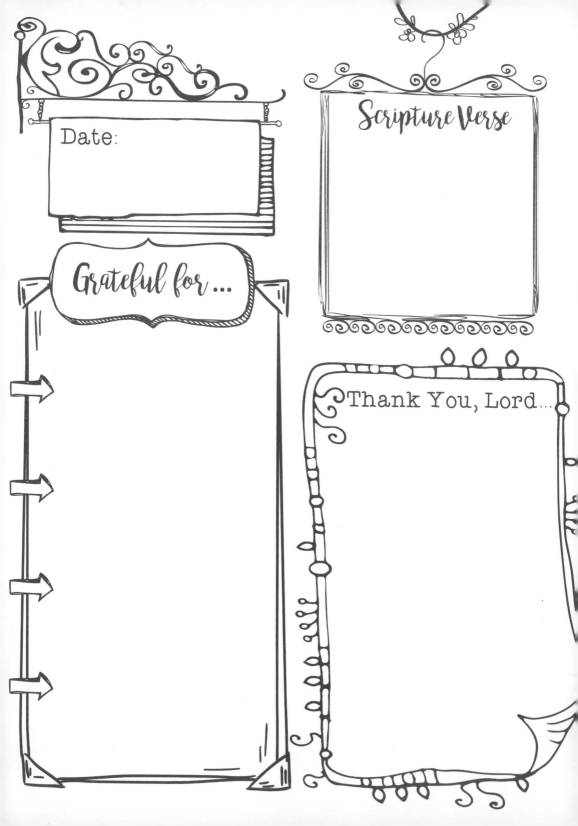

Date:

Scripture Verse

Grateful for ...

Thank You, Lord...

Date:

Scripture Verse

Grateful for ...

Thank You, Lord...

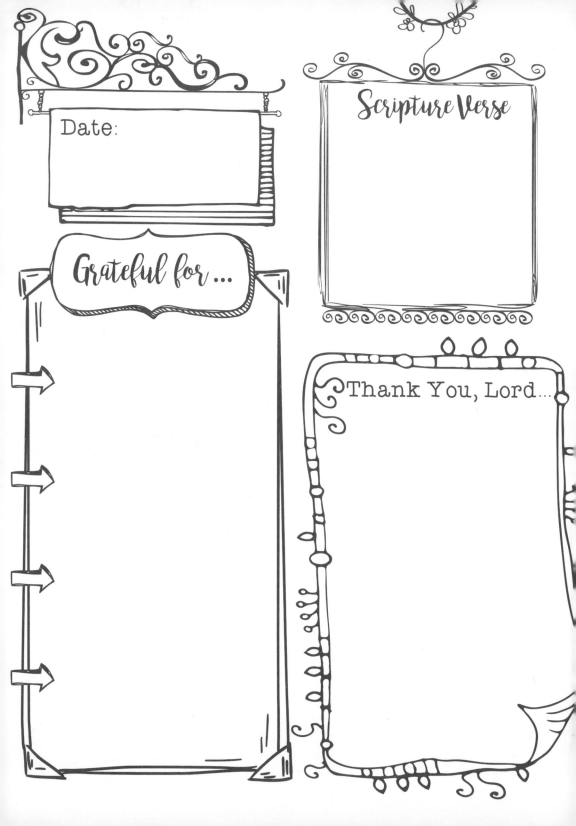

Date:

Scripture Verse

Grateful for ...

Thank You, Lord...

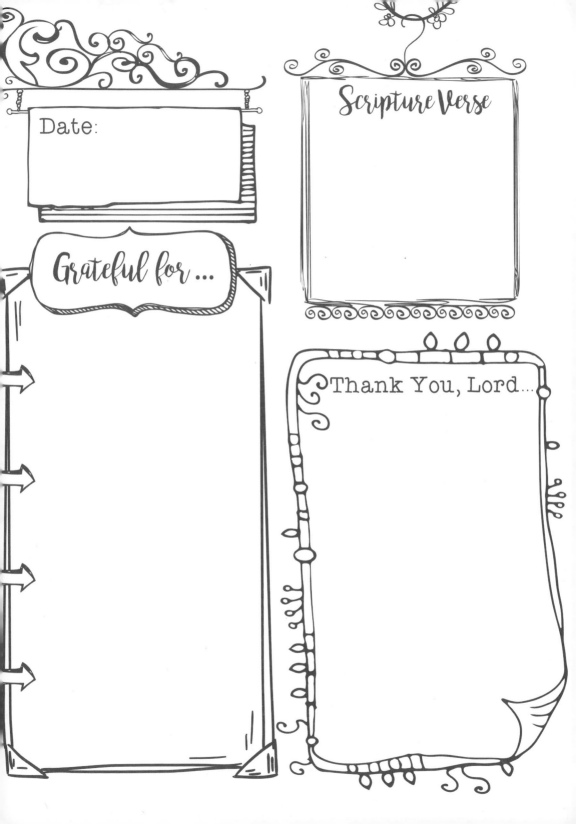

Date:

Scripture Verse

Grateful for ...

Thank You, Lord...

Date:

Scripture Verse

Grateful for ...

Thank You, Lord...

Date:

Scripture Verse

Grateful for ...

Thank You, Lord...

Date:

Scripture Verse

Grateful for ...

Thank You, Lord...

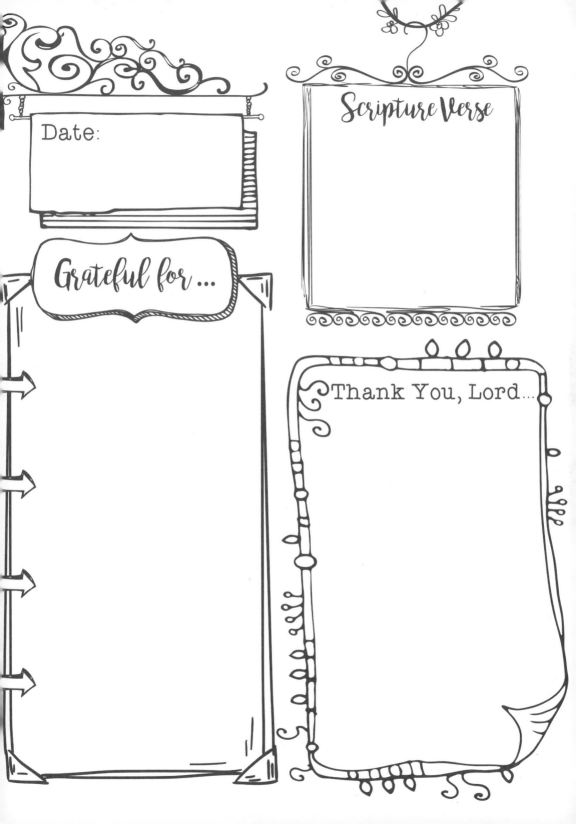

Date:

Scripture Verse

Grateful for ...

Thank You, Lord...

Date:

Scripture Verse

Grateful for ...

Thank You, Lord...

Date:

Scripture Verse

Grateful for ...

Thank You, Lord...

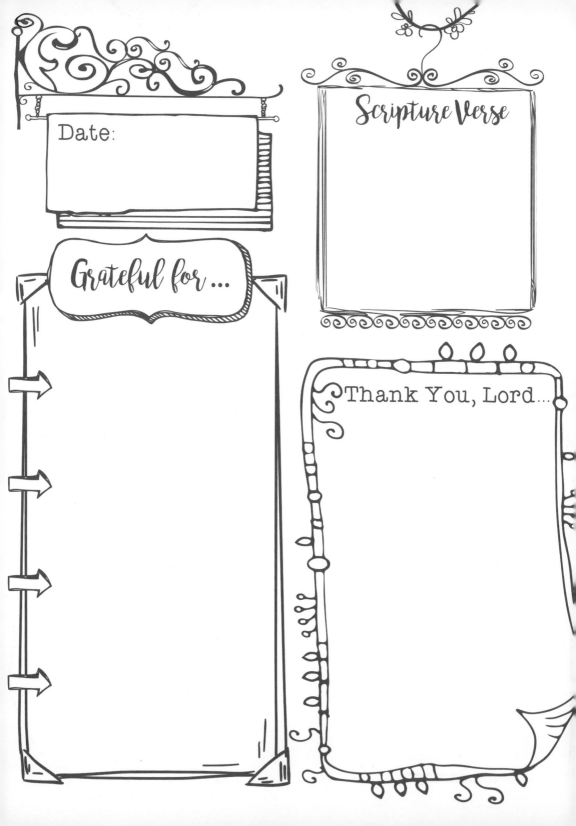

Date:

Scripture Verse

Grateful for ...

Thank You, Lord...

Date:

Scripture Verse

Grateful for ...

Thank You, Lord...

Date:

Scripture Verse

Grateful for ...

Thank You, Lord...

Date:

Scripture Verse

Grateful for ...

Thank You, Lord...

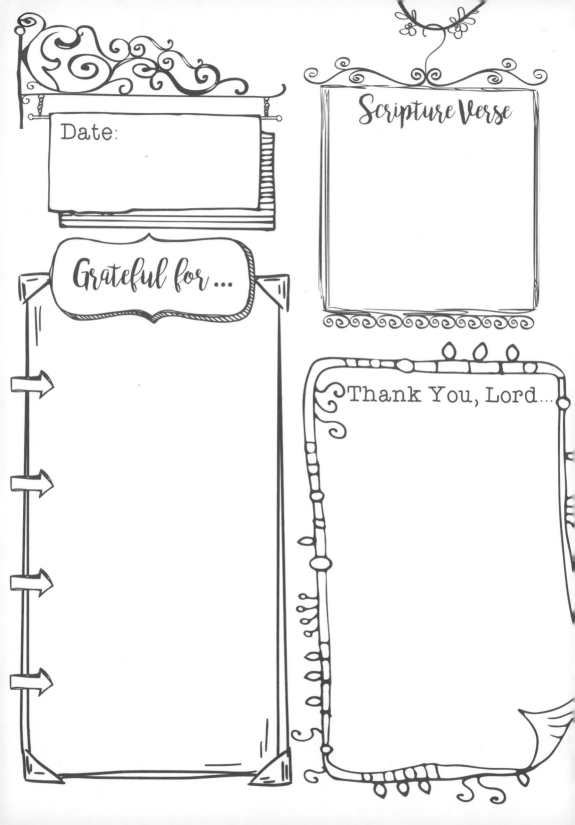

Date:

Scripture Verse

Grateful for ...

Thank You, Lord...

Date:

Scripture Verse

Grateful for ...

Thank You, Lord...

Date:

Scripture Verse

Grateful for ...

Thank You, Lord...

Date:

Scripture Verse

Grateful for ...

Thank You, Lord...

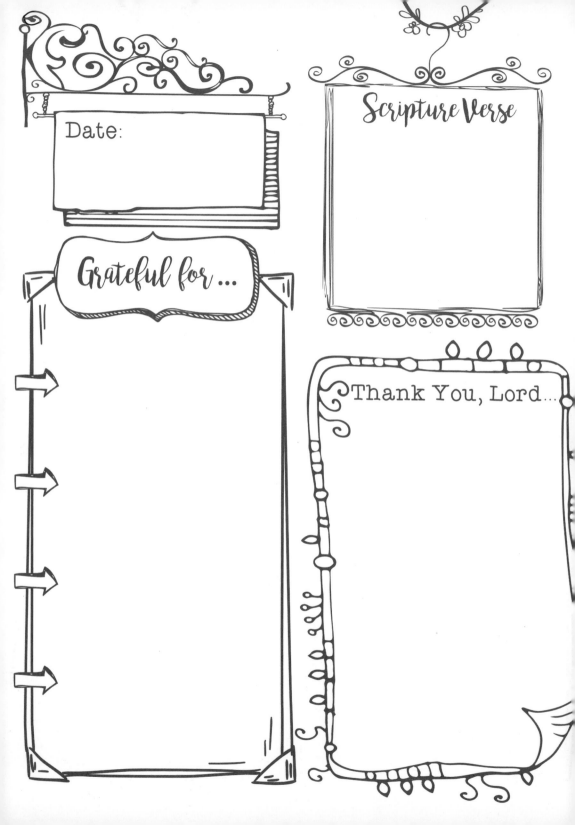

Date:

Scripture Verse

Grateful for ...

Thank You, Lord...

Date:

Scripture Verse

Grateful for ...

Thank You, Lord...

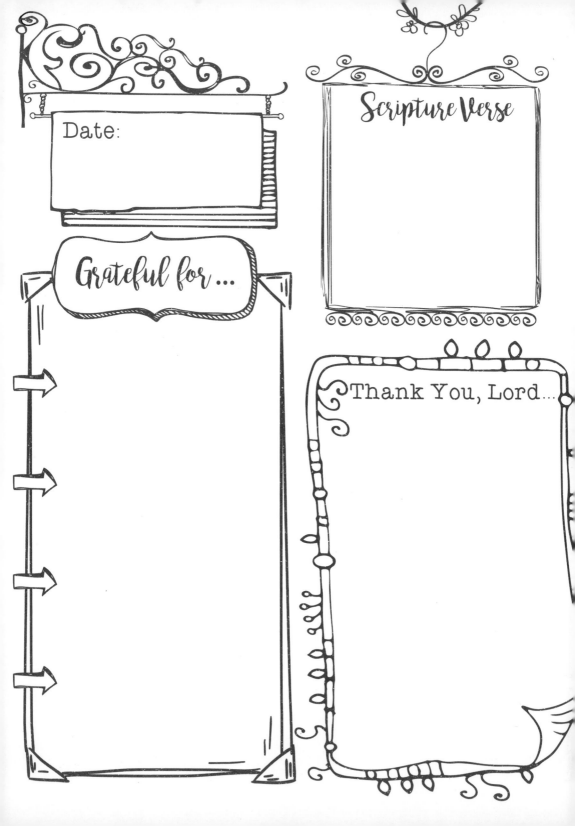

Date:

Scripture Verse

Grateful for ...

Thank You, Lord...

Date:

Scripture Verse

Grateful for ...

Thank You, Lord...

Date:

Scripture Verse

Grateful for ...

Thank You, Lord...

Date:

Scripture Verse

Grateful for ...

Thank You, Lord...

Date:

Scripture Verse

Grateful for ...

Thank You, Lord...

Date:

Scripture Verse

Grateful for ...

Thank You, Lord...

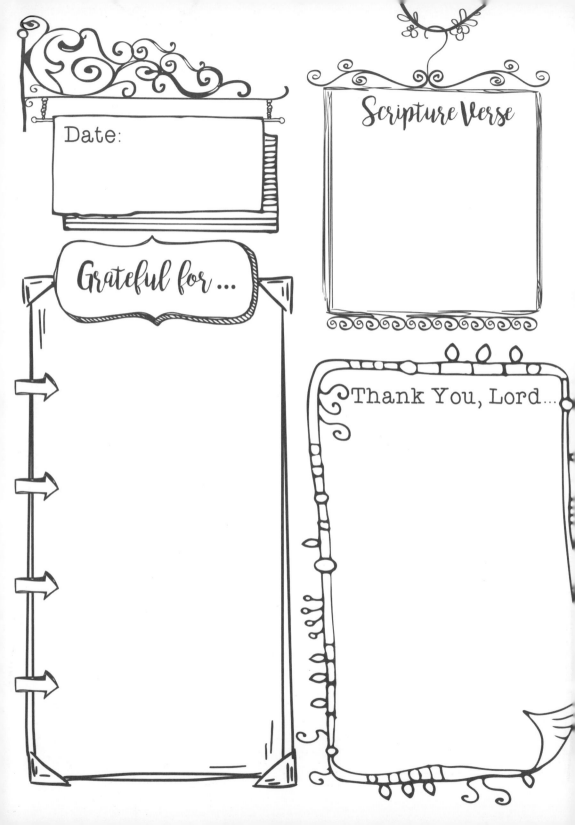

Date:

Scripture Verse

Grateful for ...

Thank You, Lord...

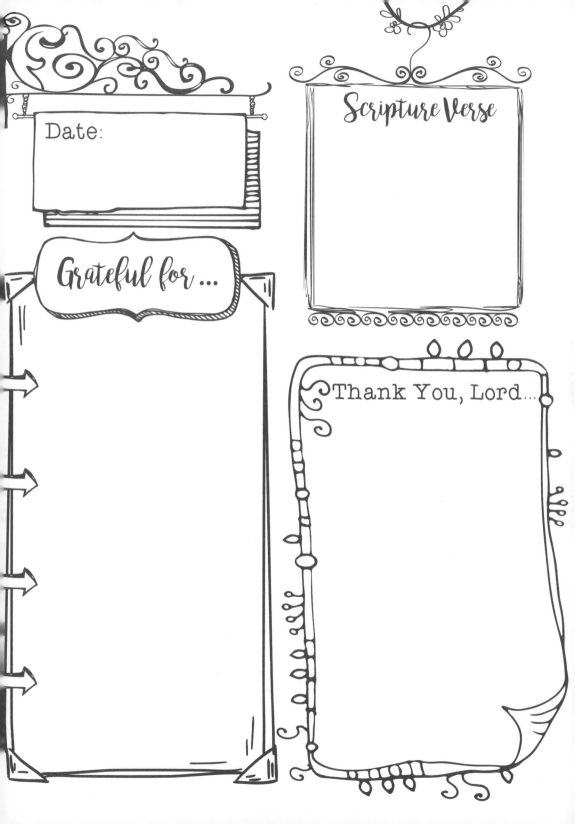

Date:

Scripture Verse

Grateful for ...

Thank You, Lord...

Date:

Scripture Verse

Grateful for ...

Thank You, Lord...

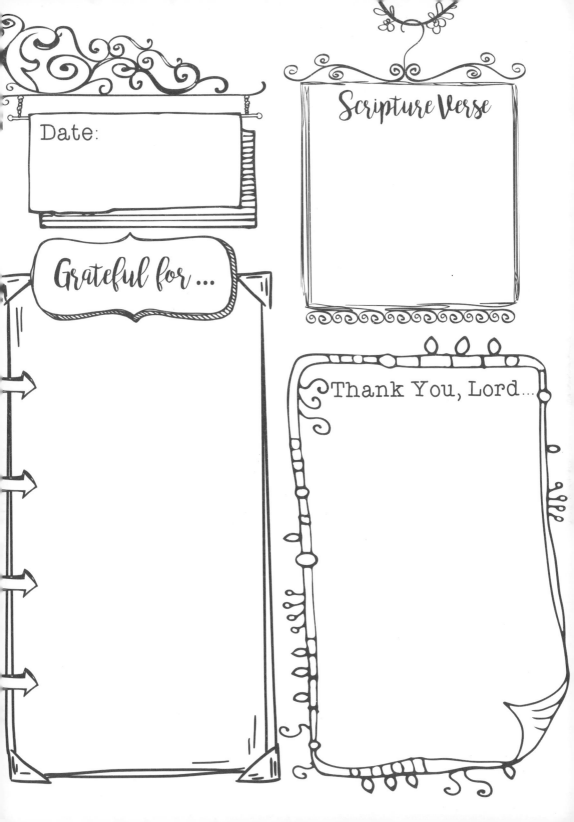

Date:

Scripture Verse

Grateful for ...

Thank You, Lord...

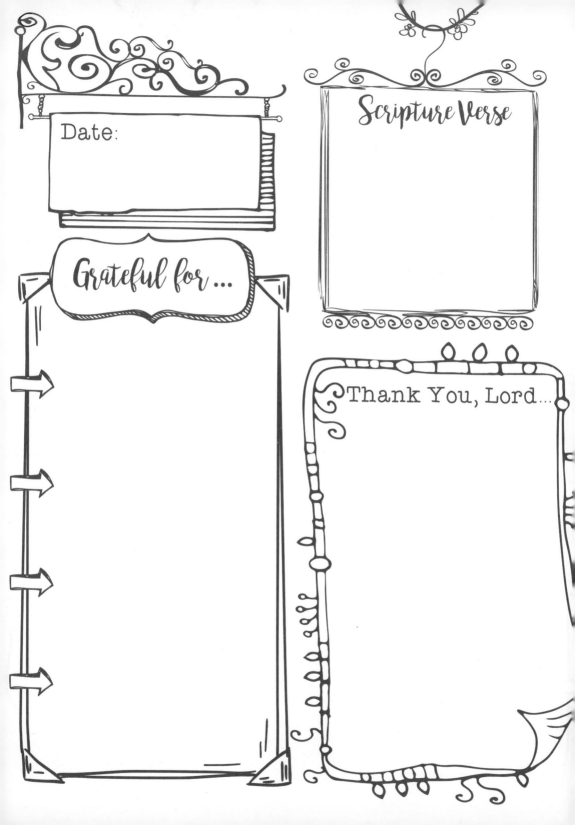

Date:

Scripture Verse

Grateful for ...

Thank You, Lord...

Date:

Scripture Verse

Grateful for ...

Thank You, Lord...

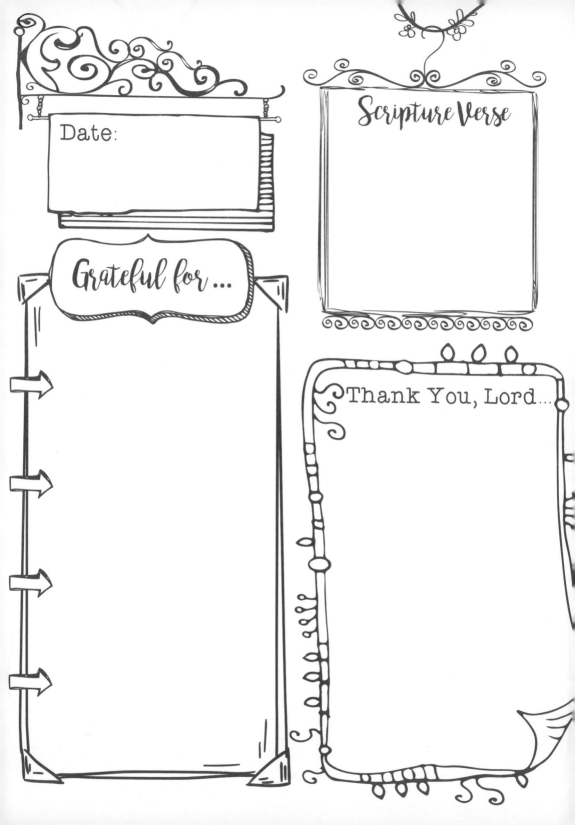

Date:

Scripture Verse

Grateful for ...

Thank You, Lord...

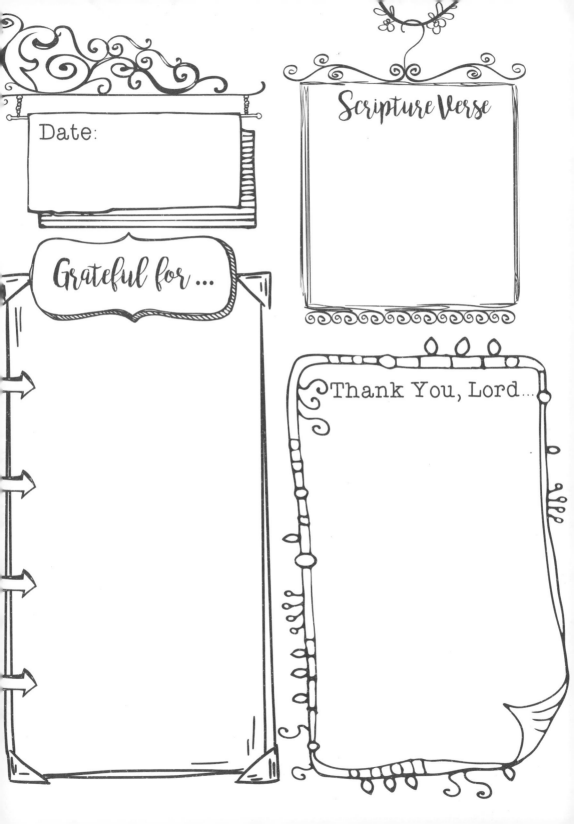

Date:

Scripture Verse

Grateful for ...

Thank You, Lord...

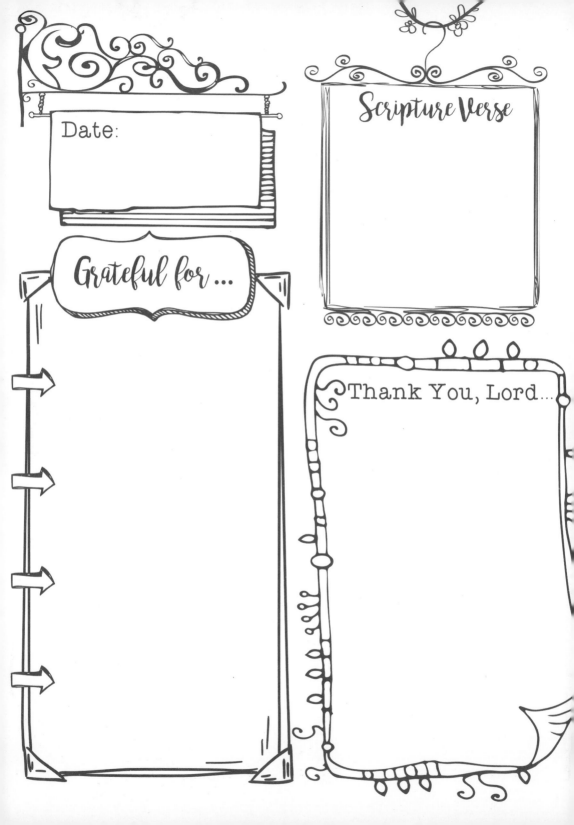

Date:

Scripture Verse

Grateful for ...

Thank You, Lord...

Date:

Scripture Verse

Grateful for ...

Thank You, Lord...

Date:

Scripture Verse

Grateful for ...

Thank You, Lord...

Date:

Scripture Verse

Grateful for ...

Thank You, Lord...

Date:

Scripture Verse

Grateful for ...

Thank You, Lord...

Date:

Scripture Verse

Grateful for ...

Thank You, Lord...

Date:

Scripture Verse

Grateful for ...

Thank You, Lord...

Date:

Scripture Verse

Grateful for ...

Thank You, Lord...

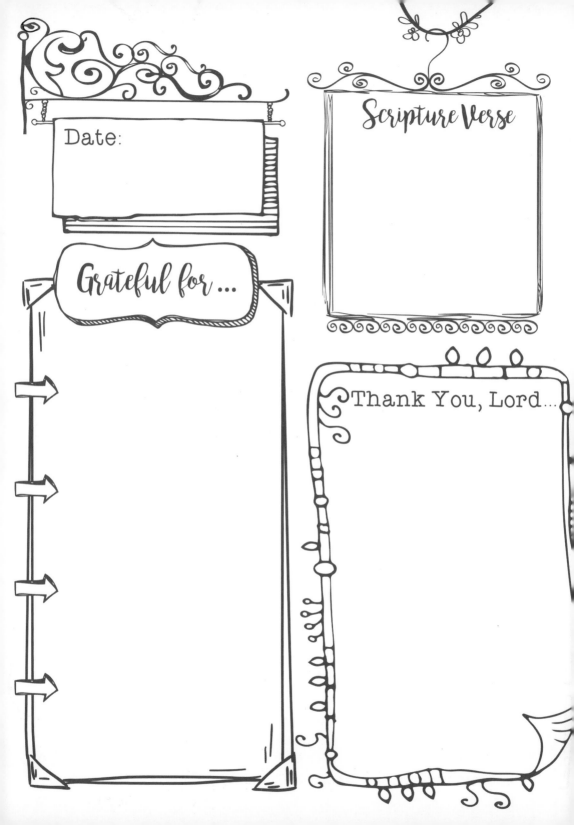

Date:

Scripture Verse

Grateful for ...

Thank You, Lord...

Date:

Scripture Verse

Grateful for ...

Thank You, Lord...

Date:

Scripture Verse

Grateful for ...

Thank You, Lord...

Date:

Scripture Verse

Grateful for ...

Thank You, Lord...

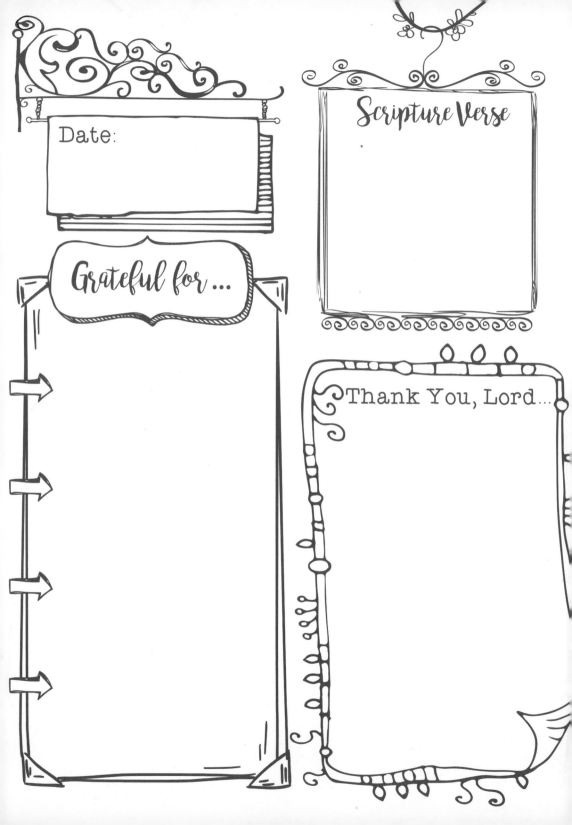

Date:

Scripture Verse

Grateful for ...

Thank You, Lord...

Date:

Scripture Verse

Grateful for ...

Thank You, Lord...

Date:

Scripture Verse

Grateful for ...

Thank You, Lord...

Date:

Scripture Verse

Grateful for ...

Thank You, Lord...

Date:

Scripture Verse

Grateful for ...

Thank You, Lord...

Date:

Scripture Verse

Grateful for ...

Thank You, Lord...

Date:

Scripture Verse

Grateful for ...

Thank You, Lord...

Date:

Scripture Verse

Grateful for ...

Thank You, Lord...

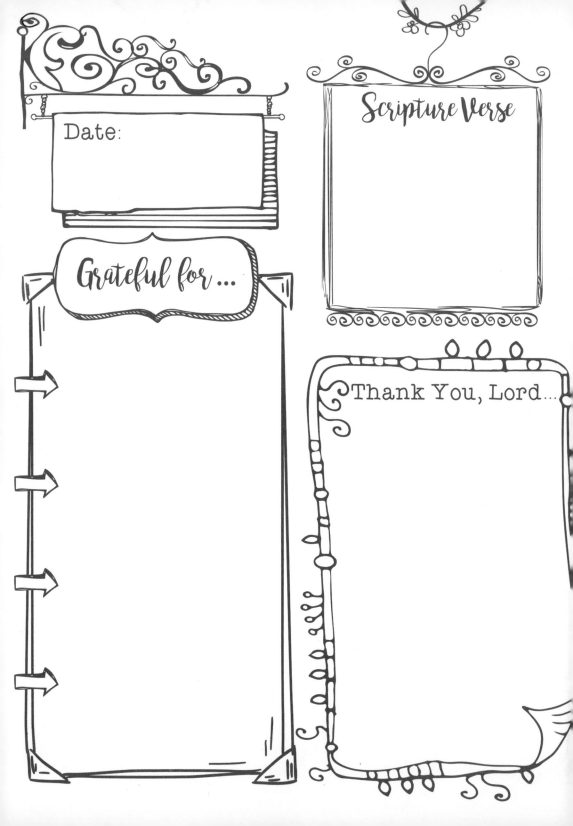

Date:

Scripture Verse

Grateful for ...

Thank You, Lord...

Date:

Scripture Verse

Grateful for ...

Thank You, Lord...

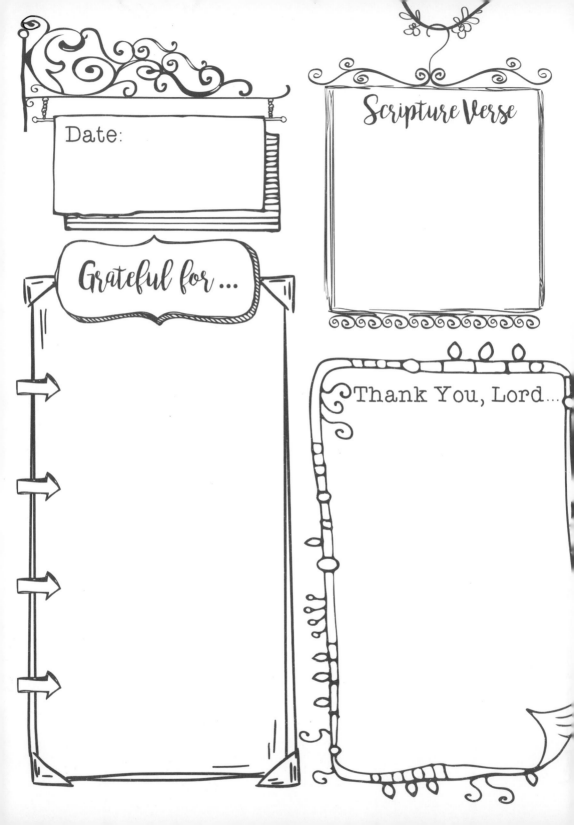

Date:

Scripture Verse

Grateful for ...

Thank You, Lord...

Date:

Scripture Verse

Grateful for ...

Thank You, Lord...

Date:

Scripture Verse

Grateful for ...

Thank You, Lord...

Date:

Scripture Verse

Grateful for ...

Thank You, Lord...

Date:

Scripture Verse

Grateful for ...

Thank You, Lord...

Date:

Scripture Verse

Grateful for ...

Thank You, Lord...

Date:

Scripture Verse

Grateful for ...

Thank You, Lord...

Date:

Scripture Verse

Grateful for ...

Thank You, Lord...

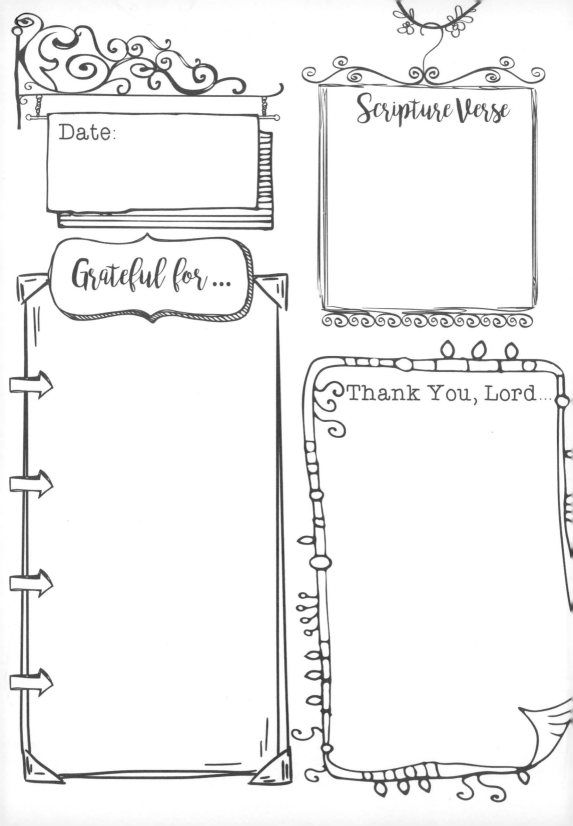

Date:

Scripture Verse

Grateful for ...

Thank You, Lord...

Date:

Scripture Verse

Grateful for ...

Thank You, Lord...

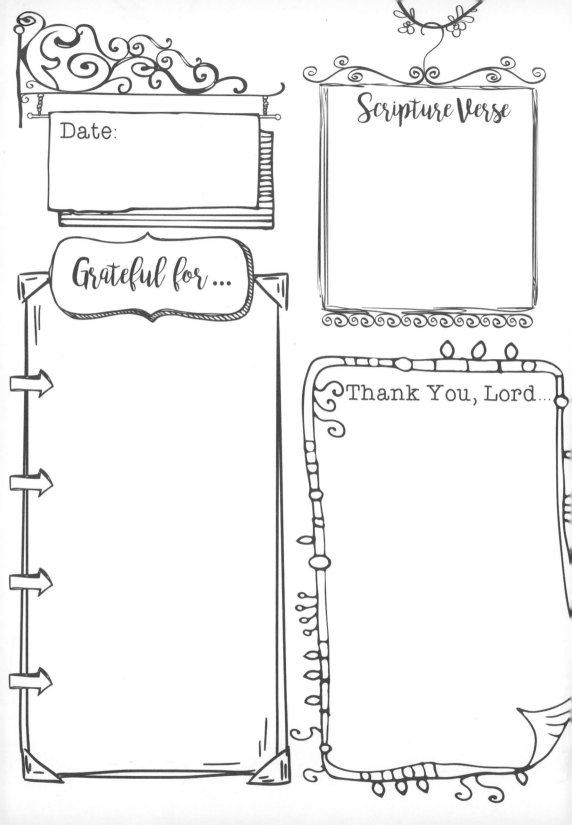

Date:

Scripture Verse

Grateful for ...

Thank You, Lord...

Date:

Scripture Verse

Grateful for ...

Thank You, Lord...

Date:

Scripture Verse

Grateful for ...

Thank You, Lord...

Date:

Scripture Verse

Grateful for ...

Thank You, Lord...

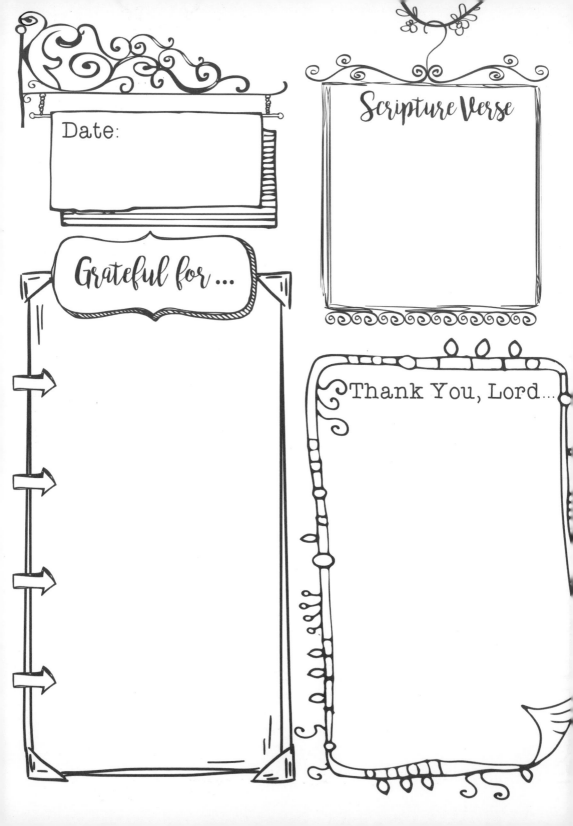

Date:

Scripture Verse

Grateful for ...

Thank You, Lord...

Date:

Scripture Verse

Grateful for ...

Thank You, Lord...

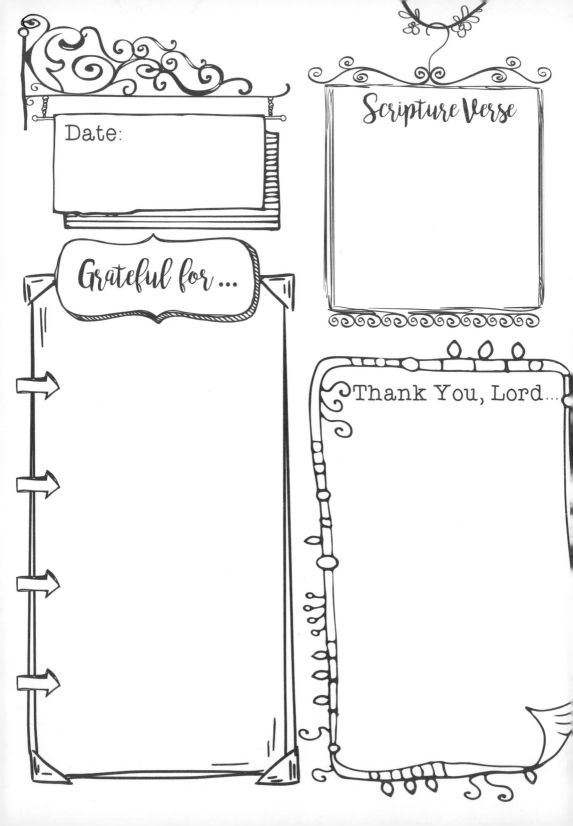

Date:

Scripture Verse

Grateful for ...

Thank You, Lord...

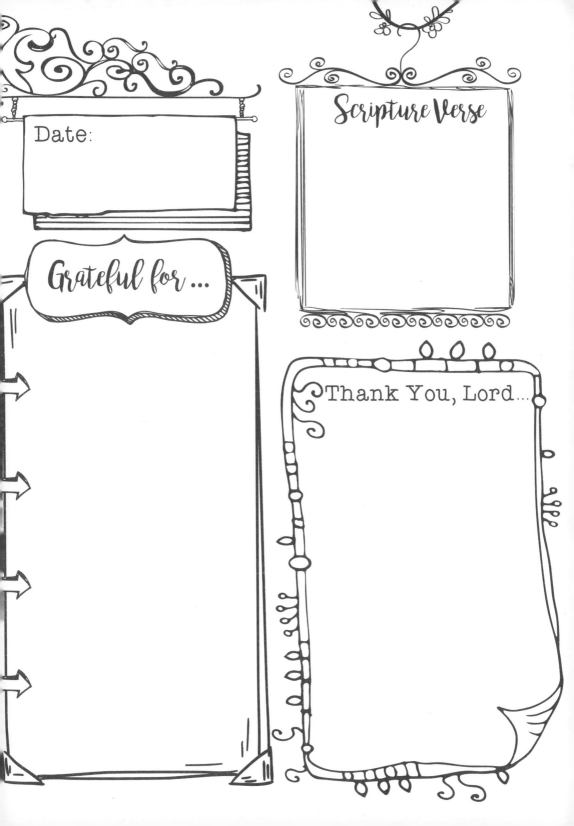

Date:

Scripture Verse

Grateful for ...

Thank You, Lord...

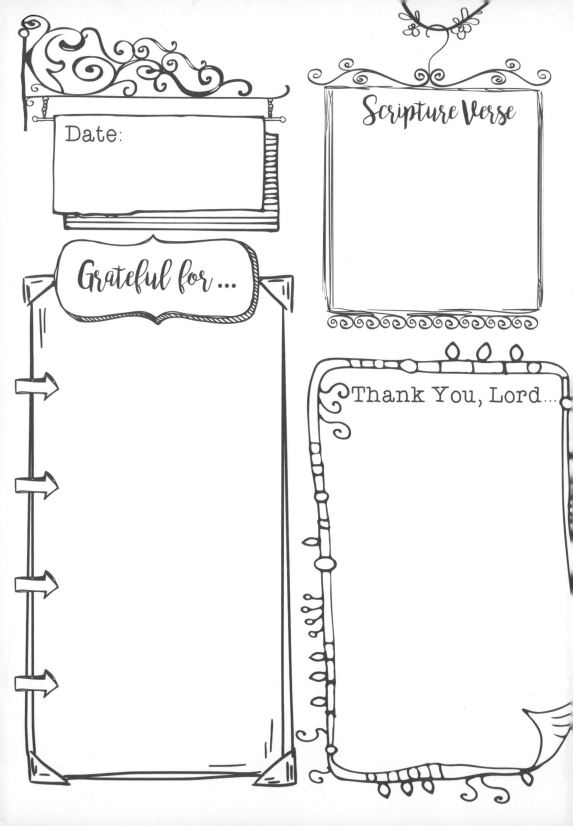

Date:

Scripture Verse

Grateful for ...

Thank You, Lord...

Date:

Scripture Verse

Grateful for ...

Thank You, Lord...

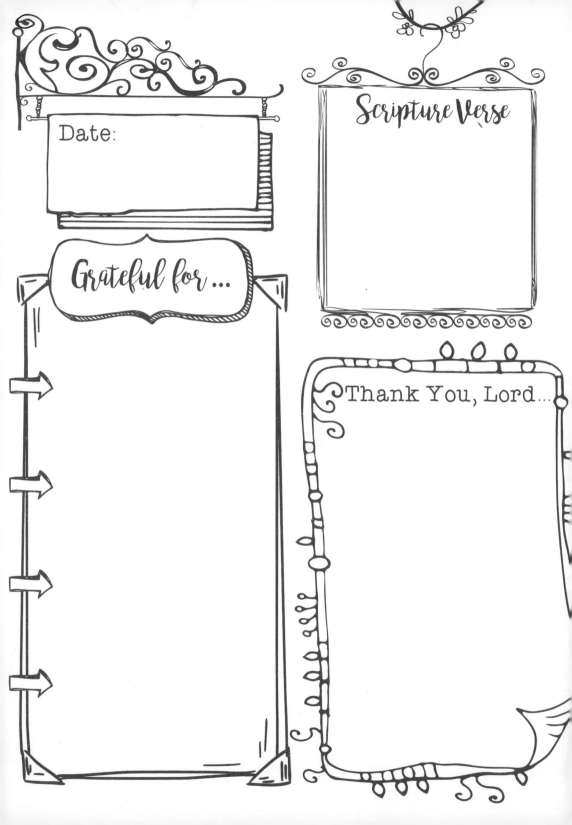

Date:

Scripture Verse

Grateful for ...

Thank You, Lord...

Date:

Scripture Verse

Grateful for ...

Thank You, Lord...

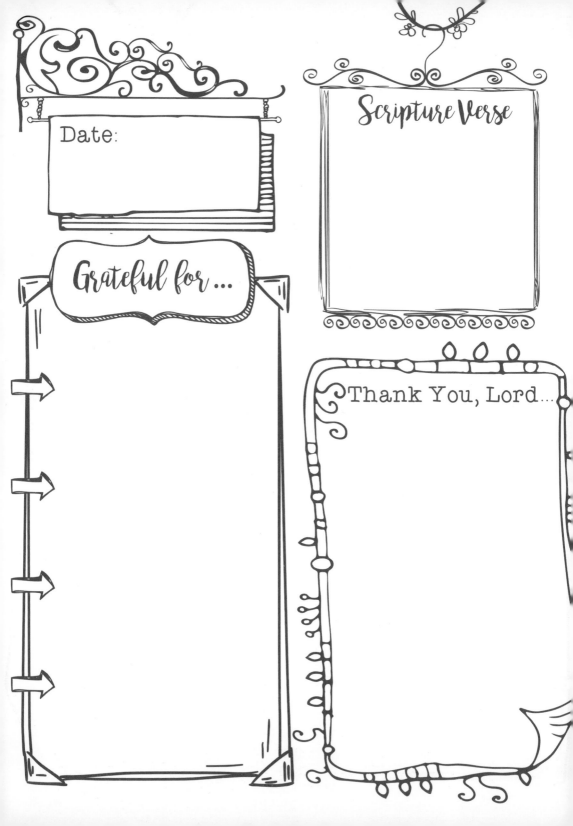

Date:

Scripture Verse

Grateful for ...

Thank You, Lord...

Date:

Scripture Verse

Grateful for ...

Thank You, Lord...

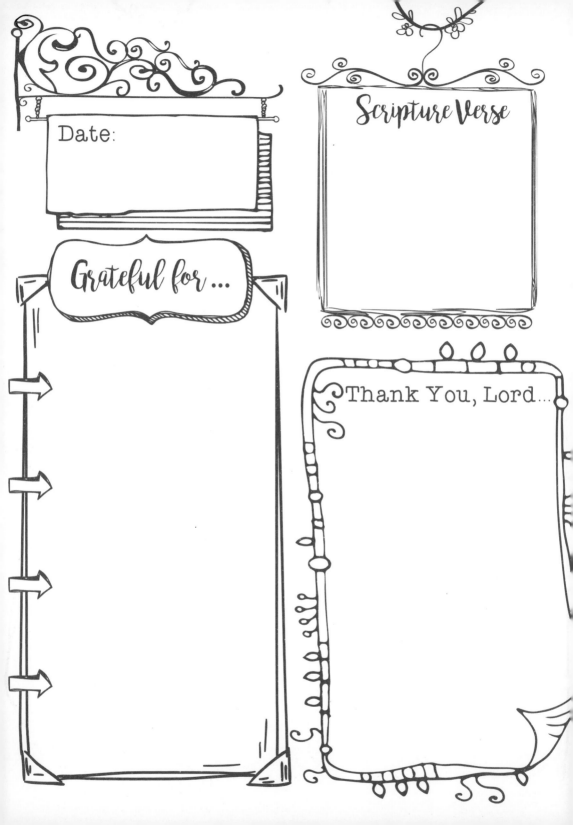

Date:

Scripture Verse

Grateful for ...

Thank You, Lord...

Date:

Scripture Verse

Grateful for ...

Thank You, Lord...

Date:

Scripture Verse

Grateful for ...

Thank You, Lord...

Date:

Scripture Verse

Grateful for ...

Thank You, Lord...

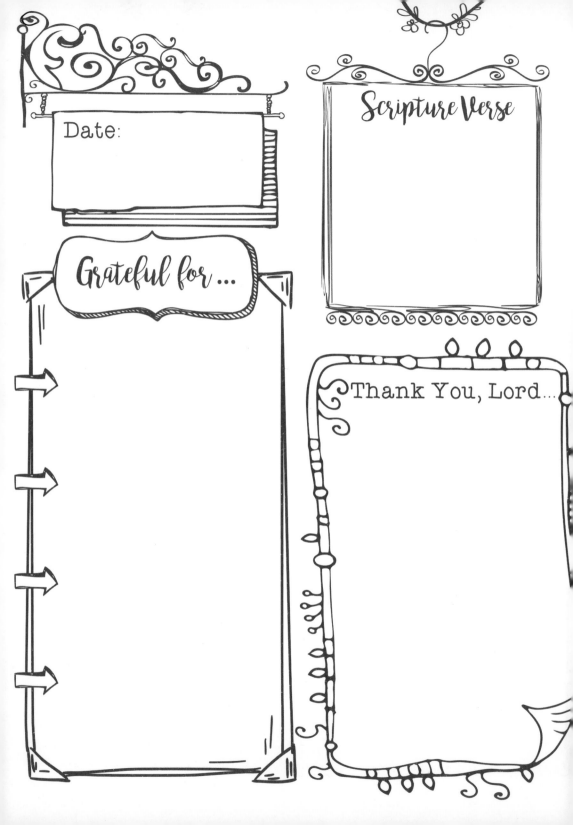

Date:

Scripture Verse

Grateful for ...

Thank You, Lord...

Date:

Scripture Verse

Grateful for ...

Thank You, Lord...

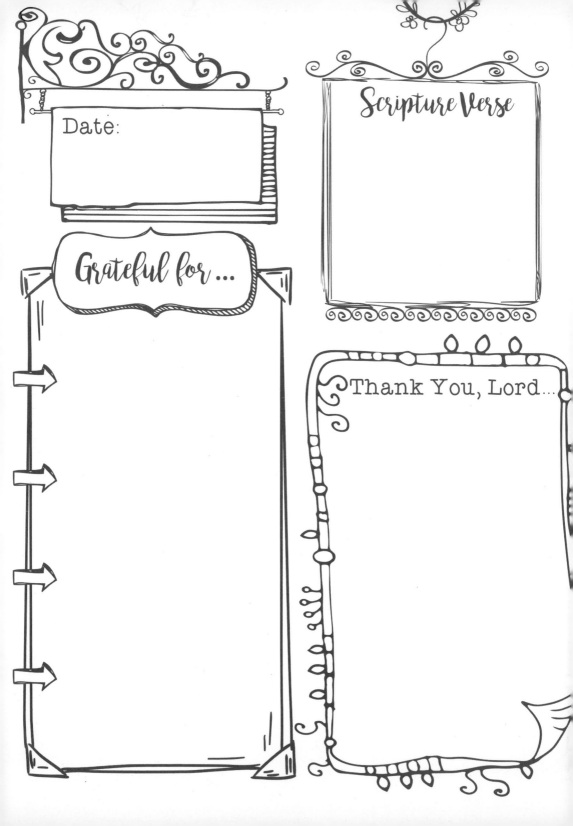

Date:

Scripture Verse

Grateful for ...

Thank You, Lord...

Date:

Scripture Verse

Grateful for ...

Thank You, Lord...

Date:

Scripture Verse

Grateful for ...

Thank You, Lord...

Date:

Scripture Verse

Grateful for ...

Thank You, Lord...

Date:

Scripture Verse

Grateful for ...

Thank You, Lord...

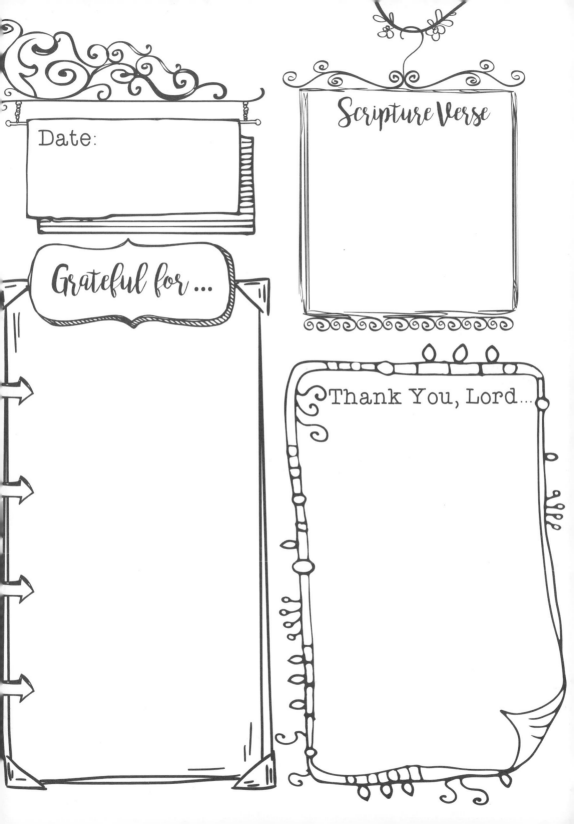

Date:

Scripture Verse

Grateful for ...

Thank You, Lord...

Date:

Scripture Verse

Grateful for ...

Thank You, Lord...

Date:

Scripture Verse

Grateful for ...

Thank You, Lord...

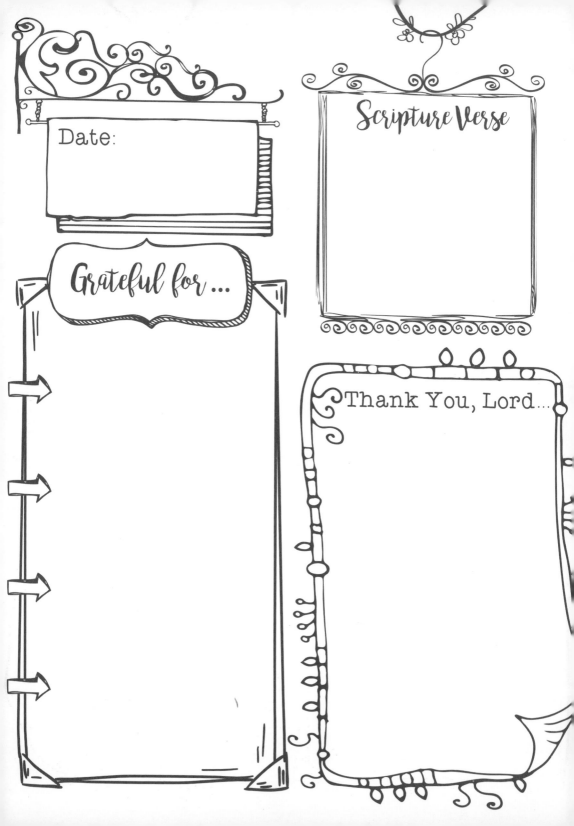

Date:

Scripture Verse

Grateful for ...

Thank You, Lord...

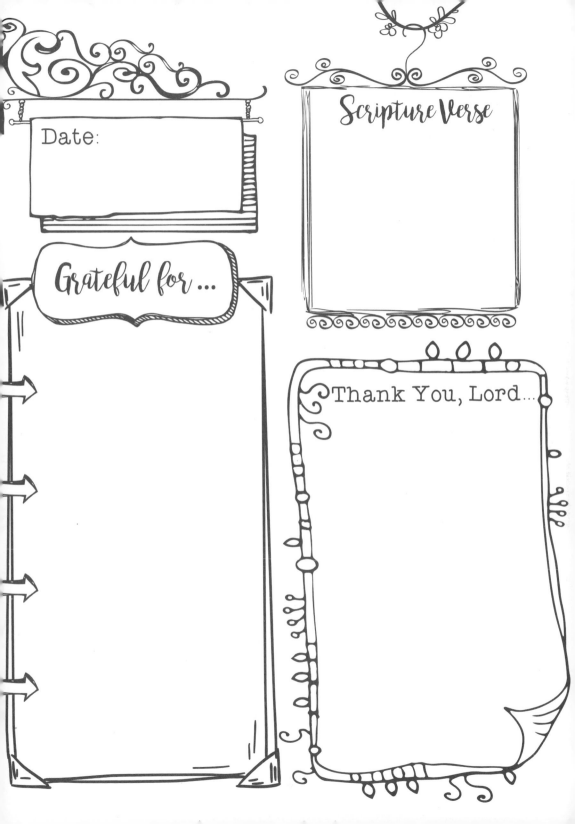

Date:

Scripture Verse

Grateful for ...

Thank You, Lord...

Date:

Scripture Verse

Grateful for ...

Thank You, Lord...

Date:

Scripture Verse

Grateful for ...

Thank You, Lord...

Date:

Scripture Verse

Grateful for ...

Thank You, Lord...

Date:

Scripture Verse

Grateful for ...

Thank You, Lord...

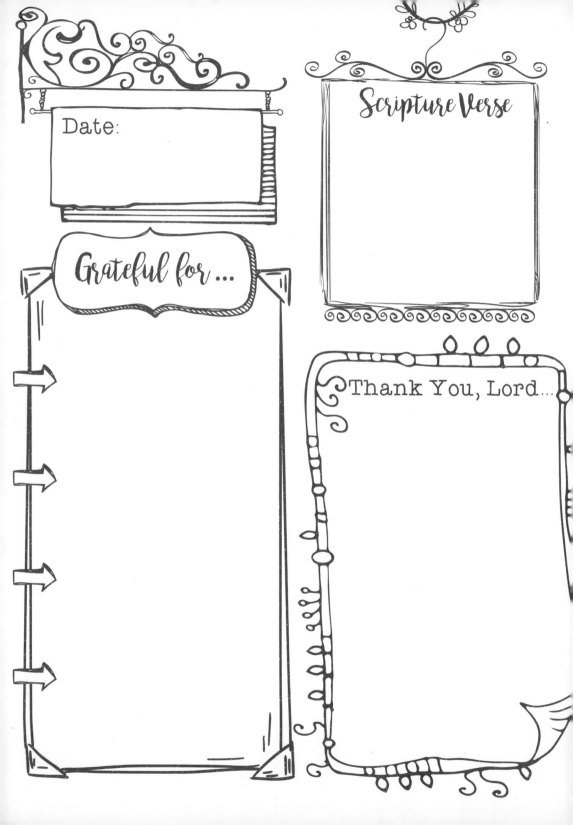

Date:

Scripture Verse

Grateful for ...

Thank You, Lord...